Four O'clock Fridays

One Man's Journey
to Become His Best Self

Alan D. Rabb with Suzy Mayer
Cover design by Kim Wayman

ISBN – 10: 1710960442

ISBN - 13: 9781710960440

Imprint: Independently published

To my wife Jill, and our two sons
whose unending love have helped and continue to
help me grow into a better person.

Contents

Preface

Part I

Chapter 1   In the Beginning

Chapter 2   Growing up

Chapter 3   The Ultimatum

Chapter 4   The Experience

Chapter 5   Beyond Creating the Vision

Part II

Chapter 6   The Journey

Chapter 7   Family

Chapter 8   Faith

Chapter 9   Fitness

Chapter 10   Fortune

Chapter 11   Fun

Chapter 12   The Sixth F

Preface

My story has been in the making for well over fifty years. At times too busy living through my life to stop long enough to find the words to share my struggles, I am now filled by the lessons I've learned along the way. I ask that you not judge me as a person and I ask that you honor the decisions I made, even knowing perhaps that you may have made different ones.

The story inscribed in the pages that follow describe the path, as I recall it, which has led me to the five principles guiding my life today. My journey is fraught with insecurity and fear, but it's also marked by moments of clear vision and confidence. Although often changing course and direction, the road is tempered by a learned determination to forge ahead even when it would be easier not to. While my path might be different from yours, like me, you are built from fragments of your past. I offer the learnings from my journey, admittedly knowing that there are literally hundreds of books with suggestions to become your best self. I developed this framework when I attended a training class; the tools and ideas created are uniquely mine.   This story is not for you to learn who I am as a person, but for you to see a glimpse of yourself in my own remembering. Some of the stories are raw. However, my intention is not to hurt or offend anyone. I am soothed by knowing that through these experiences, I have become a better husband, father and man. It is my hope that in sharing what brought me to the truths by which I have chosen to live my life, you too can gain strength and direction from my journey.

Part I

Chapter 1
In the Beginning

I have little to no recollection of a single word of praise from my parents.

From the outside, we were an average middle-class family. My dad was a salesman for a large corporation, which meant we moved around a lot. Although he always provided for his family, his career was otherwise quite unremarkable. Every morning, he'd put on one of his three suits and a freshly laundered white shirt and a tie. He'd eat breakfast while reading the newspaper and then head to work. In the evenings, he'd return home to a hot dinner, clean clothes in his drawers and closets, and his children bathed and well-behaved. He'd watch television after dinner and promptly head to bed at 10 pm so he could start his monotonous cycle all over the next morning. My mom was a stay-at-home mom and wife during my childhood. When I reached my teenage years, she worked in the banking industry, rising to a VP level, but even then, her domestic roles were clearly defined. It was the early 70s, and household duties were parsed according to gender. In short, my mom did all the work inside the house; my Dad and I took care of the yard, house repairs and other general maintenance on the outside of the house.

We celebrated all the holidays that American families typically celebrate. Christmases were chock-full of colorfully wrapped presents piled under a tree adorned with lights and sparkling tinsel. Grandparents, aunts, and uncles filled the house; the food was plentiful, the endless assortment of desserts dazzling. But there was a brokenness amongst us. We shared nothing of significance; we were strangers, all gathered because of our common DNA. The absence of any real joy left me reserved, with a feeling of isolation that ran deep. Similarly, when we spent our summers with my maternal grandparents on St. Simons Island, I spent my time fishing or walking around the island. We kids were shooed away to do whatever it is that kids do, so that our parents and grandparents could do their own thing. Longing for family connectedness, I developed surprisingly strong feelings for my grandparents. Thirsty for tenderness and appreciation, I drank up their attention, and my gratitude manifested itself in a keen sense of responsibility that caused me to look out for them when I became a young adult. It would prove to be the single-family connection I sustained.

When I was in fifth grade, I began what would become a long and passionate career as a swimmer. Aware only that I felt alive in the water, I wasn't aware of the life-long lessons I would learn through the sport. Almost immediately, my coaches demanded what felt like perfection from my body that, although long and lean, I was somewhat scrawny in strength. My efforts, however, began to pay off, and it wasn't long before I itched each day for the moment I could return to the pool. Leaving behind the dull colors of my home and the cold world of my family, the water gave me a place to focus completely on something else. I only had to concentrate on the correctness of each stroke, the width of the lane, the nearness of the next wall. The energy of my movements brought out the unpredictability and violence of the water, creating turbulent waves that crashed against the ropes. But below the surface was a stillness and serenity that fully enveloped me. Submerging myself, I existed alone; I became alive and free. These feelings fueled my passion, and even though swim practice was grueling, the water did not ask me to rely on anyone but myself to succeed. Competitive swimming offered a way to measure personal progress; I desperately needed to succeed. In the water, I knew exactly what was required of me. While continuing to push me, my coaches and teammates also praised my achievements, and this nourished me. But nothing satisfied me as much as the pure feeling of putting my shoulders under the water, lifting my feet to connect with the wall and pushing off. Surrendering my body, focusing my mind on the end, doing nothing but experiencing, engaging, pushing myself. Being fully in the race. Being in the moment.

Swimming consumed my life, leaving little time for anything else. My parents threatened to take away the privilege of swimming if I didn't keep up my grades or complete my household chores. I remember studying for exams by putting notecards full of facts inside plastic baggies and attaching them at the end of the lane where I'd look at them, memorizing them as I swam back to the other end of the pool. It was the only way I could manage both decent grades and swimming. Even though I was on a team, I had no real friends to speak of; if I wasn't in the pool, I was at home studying, sleeping, mowing the lawn or doing some other assigned chore. I was reliant on my parents both for transportation and for their financial support. They never let me forget that I needed them and held this power over my head as a way to get what they wanted. Although they always pushed me to do more and better, I wonder what my success really meant to them. Whatever I did, however much I succeeded, they were never satisfied, and they never failed to remind me that there was always room for improvement. This dissatisfaction would have lifelong effects of things "never being good enough." Winning one of my first races, I recall my Dad's words: "You had a slow start." I learned not to look to them for encouragement or affirmation. Branded in my brain to this day is the memory of one of my final wins. There was the euphoric moment I pulled up from the water and, searching the leaderboard, saw my name at the top. Ecstatic, I began pumping my fist in the air. My parents were watching in the stands. When I came out to meet them, my dad said, "You could have done better; it wasn't your personal best." With those words, something died inside me. In its place, a defiance was born, with the knowledge that pleasing myself was all that really mattered.

When I was sixteen, as a fairly new driver, I was on my way to swim practice on a dark March afternoon. It was damp and foggy outside. A dog ran into the street; swerving to avoid it, my car instead hit a telephone pole. Fraught with terror that I might have killed someone's pet, my heart racing and my stomach sick, I didn't immediately know that I also had a broken elbow and jaw, a fractured knee, and a severe concussion. Later that day, my dad met me at the hospital, furious. Not asking how I was, he said only, "Why didn't you hit the f****** dog, this was a brand-new car." Those were the last words he spoke to me for six weeks. He took away my license and made me sit for the SAT exams the next day, concussion and all. I retreated further into myself and endured.

Chapter 2
Growing Up

If my parents taught me inadvertently how to survive on my own, it was my wife who taught me how to love. When I met Jill in 1984, my black and white colorless world tilted on its side and a whole palette of color was introduced. It wasn't that ours was a fairy tale romance of love-at-first sight, in which the moment I saw her I knew I was meeting my future wife. We were friends first, colleagues really, since we were both among the fifty-eight employees who joined the same company on the same day. She was nineteen and I was twenty-one. We were each involved in other relationships, and we even found ourselves double dating on multiple occasions. But something changed when, more than a year after we had first met, we both found ourselves single. Jill suddenly looked different to me. She hadn't changed her hair or makeup or her style of dress. The possibility of something more than friendship charged through my body, and Cupid was lurking around the corner. Two years later, just nine months after we started dating, we were engaged to be married. Less than a year after the engagement, we tied the knot.

We were young and had a lot of growing up to do. I had been shaped to travel the conventional path, which meant that my imagined future held kids, nice cars, and houses of increasing size and value. Never being satisfied was an ambition my parents instilled in me; their attainment of one thing after the other was their main source of happiness, and a belief to which I ascribed. Not knowing anything else, I too believed in this American dream. I remember working what felt like endless hours to put money in the bank. Although Jill and I both had salaried full-time jobs, on weekends, we'd clear out whatever unnecessary possessions we could find, load them in the trunk of the car, and head to a flea market to sell what we could. I painted houses on the weekend. Jill started a catering company, baking specialty cakes for sale at gift fairs and private parties. We were driven.

I was an expert at trekking the straight path piloted by step-by-step tasks. I knew how to budget. I had spreadsheets that separated funds into different accounts, with savings categories for gifts, vacations, retirement, household expenses and upgrades, future kids. We had schedules that indicated what days of the week we would vacuum, grocery shop, change the linens, dust the furniture. I had a list in the garage that indicated which car needed to be serviced when. I liked routine, and playing house and planning our future was squarely in my comfort zone. Although my willingness to participate in organizing our life was an admirable skill, and one for which my wife was grateful, the longer we were together, the more difficult it became to connect in a less practical, more emotional way.

Jill lived at home when we met. This meant that, although I had my own place, we spent a lot of time with my soon-to-be in-laws. I was taken aback by the ease with which they communicated. I could easily talk about my job, the job industry as a whole, and even what I believed about politics. During the first Thanksgiving we were together,

Jill's family remained at the table for over two hours after eating, simply having a conversation. An hour after we left the table, I couldn't tell you what was discussed. It felt like all the words were tripping over themselves in my mind, as each family member told anecdotes from their week, shared about something they had read, or even gossiped about some celebrity. I didn't contribute much, but instead shifted my weight from leg to leg as I tried to hide my awkwardness and disquiet. Absent were the long silences or discreet quips in the semblance of communication that had infected holiday dinners while growing up. I'm certain that Jill's parents and brother found it odd that I was so quiet; perhaps they were even silently disappointed in Jill's choice of a partner. Over years of marriage, I came to expect and even to engage, to some extent, in these long hours of talking and constant daily communication. Until recently, I really struggled to feel at home in a conversation whose only intention is to bring the speakers closer together.

Of course, when my and Jill's friendship-turned-romance was first budding, the words and stories came easily. As a new couple falling in love, we talked about everything: favorite television shows, school, our families. We revealed likes and dislikes of restaurants and foods, ideas and experiences. We dreamt about future houses, vacations, kids. We shared all this on dates, over dinner in a hundred different restaurants, on vacations, and while visiting friends. In those days, we did not lack for things to do or words to share.

Early in our marriage, balancing our very different families flowed naturally. Jill continued to talk to her mom multiple times a week, and we saw my parents every Sunday for dinner. We were each, individually and as a couple, continuing with the patterns that had long been formed. As I struggled with my discomfort watching conversations flow effortlessly with Jill's family, she wrestled with the absence of energy and tenderness with my family. Jill's family was loving; mine was cordial. On those rare occasions when our families joined together, the air grew thick with tension and heavy with falseness. It wasn't long before my family's snide comments put a wedge between my parents and Jill and me.

As my relationship with my family was growing more and more sour, my relationship with Jill's parents seemed to be deepening. My father-in-law began to embrace me as part of his family. He spent hours teaching me the things I had never learned—how to change a tire, check the brakes in our cars, and other requirements of general car maintenance. He taught me how to do plumbing. He didn't teach only specific skills, but he taught me that I could learn to do almost anything, rather than hiring someone else. He helped me finish our basement by teaching me how to properly wire electrical outlets and lights. He always had time for me. He always *made* the time for me. I began to understand how this generosity of his, and my willingness to receive, created not only a mutual respect but a sense of ease and intimacy in each other's company.

After five years of marriage, we grew our family: our first son was born. The different rhythms of our relationships with our parents continued to deepen as they became grandparents. Unsurprisingly, Jill's parents received more updates about our newest family member, because we were in closer contact with them. When my parents sent our son a gift, they would sign the card, "From your other grandparents." Their jealousy manifested itself in strange ways; rather than trying to see us or call for updates more frequently, they turned their resentment into hurtful comments and actions. They stopped acknowledging my birthday. On the rare occasions when they called, if Jill answered the phone, they simply asked "Is Alan there?" When our son was a year and a half, my parents and I essentially stopped talking, although it would be another year until we completed what I've always called my parental divorce. During that year, I tried to mend their pain and mine. Jill and I sent Christmas gifts and cards to my parents. They were returned unopened. My parents have never met our second child, born four years later.

Because we were raised so differently, being parents together created unexpected challenges. To this day, I believe my parents tried to do what they suspected were the "right things" but the dysfunction in my family created lasting marks. However, I saw other families growing up, and I was a good student, so I learned well. I had a strong idea of what was expected of me. I coached baseball, became the boys' swim team treasurer, attended school activities and conferences, and volunteered in community events. It wasn't that I didn't **want** to do these things, I needed to learn **how** to do these things. I wanted to be a supportive Dad. Admittedly, engaging completely was at times difficult, and I was by no means perfect; I simply did the best I could. A chord was struck, however, when my oldest son was old enough to join Cub Scouts. Jill talked to me about signing him up. I had been a Boy Scout and my Dad was an Eagle Scout, so I felt a personal connection to the integrity and virtuosity implicit in the organization. The evening of the meeting, my son and I ate an early dinner, buckled ourselves into the car and drove the short distance to the planning meeting for the new troop. We walked into the church building along with a gaggle of other boys and dads, all intent on the mission of creating men out of young sons. The first speaker, a dad and a former Eagle Scout himself, talked about the logistics of the organization, how the groups were organized, and what was expected in terms of attendance and participation, all the while touting the merits and value of being a Boy Scout. Next, a young teen got up and spoke about what Boy Scouts meant to him, about the lessons he learned as each badge was earned, about the camaraderie and the closeness he felt to his dad when they did their overnight campouts and such. As he rambled on, my heart began to race. I felt weak, and my ears began to close in until the sound was muffled. I got dizzy; my fingers started to tingle. I was having a full-fledged panic attack. I waited for the young speaker to sit down, told my son I wasn't feeling well, and we fled. As we drove the short distance home, I assured him in between heavy breaths that I was okay and just needed to lie down. I walked into the house and straight upstairs to our bathroom. Alone, I felt myself shift to the young boy I was back in New Jersey. As a cub scout, I was being hounded to get one badge and then, immediately focus on the next and the next and the next until all that mattered was the amount of space left on the merit badge sash. Coming back to myself, I knew then that I couldn't participate again in that empty reward system, and I realized that, this time around, I was free from obligation. Neither of my boys would become scouts. Looking back, I wish I had been able to better understand and reconcile my childhood feelings because it took precedence over what might have been best for my boys.

By now, it was the mid-nineties, and, despite the Cub Scout hiccup, I thought I was doing it all. I was growing my career, actively participating in my kids' lives, volunteering in community events. My kids had a thriving relationship with their maternal grandparents and seemed not to feel the absence of a relationship with my parents. I was enjoying a lack of stress. I imagine the break with my parents had impacted me, as evidenced by my panic attack, but at this time these effects didn't seem to disturb me. Feeling that I was riding high in my life, especially in my career, I unconsciously began pulling away from my wife and boys, chasing ambition. The "never being satisfied" emotion was tugging at me. My career started to take precedence over my family. With pain I admit that when Jill was pregnant with our second child, I moved to Los Angeles for six months for a short-term assignment at work. I left her to handle the house, my oldest son, and the pregnancy on her own. It was all about my career and my driving need to advance my career. I didn't know it, but I had lost sight of what mattered.

Although my vision was blurred, Jill's was clear as day. She knew that if I could not commit to her and the kids, she was better off without me. One evening in the middle of February, as the wind whipped around my feet, I rushed into the house, and slammed the front door shut. "It's freezing out there," I commented when I noticed Jill sitting on the couch, looking through a magazine. She did not even raise her eyes in my direction. "What's the matter with you?" I quipped. I was met with silence. "Hello," I repeated. "You just don't get it," Jill quietly said, shaking her head. And then with tears of rage streaming down her face, she said, "If I don't have your job tattooed in the middle of my forehead, you don't pay attention to me. You look right through me. You haven't been home to put the kids to bed in weeks. Your life is only about work. If I'm going to be a single mother, then I can do it without you." And then she said the words that changed my life.

"I want a divorce."

Chapter 3
The Ultimatum

The February storm I had escaped only moments before was nothing compared to the storm that was now unleashed inside my life. I could be certain that, by morning, the sky outside would be clear again. But I did not have the same hope for that chaos which stirred within me.

Jill's message was, I confess, not unfamiliar. She had voiced her dissatisfaction dozens of times, but I had relegated it to that category of background noise, clearly unaware of its significance. This time was different, of that I was certain. I had ignored her for too long.

I knew that my drive for career success, though ingrained at an early age, was only in motion because I wanted to provide for the very family I might now lose. This thought made me frantic. Take my family out of the equation, and my drive was completely deflated; what sat in front of me instead would be an empty office, an empty home, an empty goal.

I was scared, but I was also somewhat stumped. Although I could hear Jill's anger and knew it was real, I still struggled to fully understand what Jill was telling me. I couldn't make sense of the concepts. I thought striving for a successful career was the expectation. It wasn't that I didn't want to change, it's that I didn't comprehend where the change needed to happen. Nothing in my background gave me the tools or experience I needed to understand how to fix this situation.

I had always known how to make a step-by-step plan to get where I wanted to be. But my careful, methodical tools were useless now. Connecting with Jill and the family in the way I needed to wasn't anything like trying to improve my swim time by fifteen seconds. It felt more like I had to improve my time in a pool that had no walls. Jill was smart enough to know that she couldn't expect complete and immediate transformation from me, and she never pretended to ask for that. She wanted this to work.

She was willing to accept baby steps, small changes. When I admitted to her that I didn't understand what she expected, she replied simply, "Have dinner one night a week with us as a family. We can start small and work on this together."

Looking back on that conversation, I realize, with shame, how difficult I made acquiescing to that small request. Even after she asked, I angled for a negotiation. "I can be home at six on Fridays" I told her. With straight conviction, she informed me that that wouldn't be early enough. After rather pathetically continuing to try to negotiate with her, I finally understood that she would not accept anything less than my promise to be home for dinner every Friday night, no exceptions. I agreed at last to leave work at four o'clock on Fridays, to get a jump on the traffic. Thus, four o'clock Fridays came into being. I blocked my calendar from 4 pm onward every single Friday for the remainder of the year, and by doing so, four o'clock Fridays became somehow sanctified, an unbudgeable commitment I was making to my own life. As the hour approached each Friday, I learned to promptly shut down my computer, or excuse myself from any meeting, even if it was running over, and head to my car to make the long drive home. Every time, I would arrive no later than 5 pm. This was what a new beginning looked like.

***

Months later, I arrived early for a meeting with one of our franchise partners. Although I traveled frequently, and there was nothing unique about this meeting, the visit would bring changes I had no way of anticipating. With a couple of hours to spare before the formal meeting began, the finance controller, who I will call Ken for purposes here, suggested, "Let's take a walk." As we strolled through the bottling facility, Ken said hello by name to the dozens of people we saw. Some were in his organization, some worked in other areas. He stopped and chatted with a few, asking about their families, their recent vacation, their latest half-marathon. I watched in awe at his casual, friendly style. His office was replete with photos of his parents, of his kids and wife, and there he was: smack in the middle of them all. He had a poem on his wall written by one of his kids and a framed collage of photos with the catchphrase "Best Dad" placed behind his desk. Jill's words, "You just don't get it," played over and over in my mind, haunting me.

I summoned my courage and, once we were in the privacy of his office, asked Ken, "How do you balance home, family, and work and still manage to say hello and know what matters to the seventy-five people in your organization?" I went on to share, for the first time ever with someone other than Jill, the struggles of my marriage. I didn't even know Ken that well, but it seemed that the timing and the setting were ripe at that moment for me to open up, to seek help.

When I was done saying all I could, Ken sat quietly looking at me. He didn't ask questions. He didn't comment on anything I said. I wondered, awkwardly, if he had even heard me at all. Then, slowly he reached into his pocket and, taking out his wallet, he pulled out a notecard and handed it to me. On the card were ten bullets, separated into two sections.

GRATEFUL	EXCITED
1.)	1.)
2.)	2.)
3.)	3.)
4.)	4.)
5.)	5.)

"This is how I focus," he said. "Each week, I list five things on each side of the card. It keeps me grounded," was all he revealed. I tried to make sense of the underlined words that appeared to represent each of the two categories: "Grateful. Excited."

As I turned these words over in my mind, Ken said gently, "I think you should sign up for a leadership program I did many years ago with this company (which again, from here on, I'll name) *Empowerment*." He paused for a moment then said, "I think it would help you immensely." Ken didn't say much more, and he didn't tell me about his personal story that day, but somehow from his pauses, from the gaps between his words, I got the distinct impression that he was sharing something very precious to him. I felt like he was communicating that he too had struggled. He too had lost his way. And in that moment, I felt a glimmer of hope, something I desperately needed.

Chapter 4
The Experience

I didn't know, when I arrived in Reno, Nevada after a long week at work, that the weekend's Empowerment experience would be full of extremes that would shake my life, both personally and professionally. I arrived as I did for every training I attended: with notebook in hand, two pairs of khakis and collared shirts, the book I was reading, and my phone and phone charger, ready to keep in touch as always.

We gathered in a small white-walled room in a rundown strip mall just outside of town. The room reminded me of an insurance office well past its prime, replete with an old Mr. Coffee machine and stacks of Styrofoam cups. I sat in one of the blue plastic shell chairs with wood Eiffel legs, feeling very aware of the bright white florescent lights shining on the scuffed walls. As I sat, a woman likely in her mid-thirties approached and handed me a medium-sized blue paper gift bag with paper handles, and then walked away. Baffled, I scanned the contents of the bag. Inside was a bag of potato chips, some loose hard candy, a bottle of water, a snickers bar and a stress ball. A small gift card was enclosed with the words, "Enjoy the weekend, I know you'll gain a lot." It was signed "Ken."

The other participants entered the room, looking as bewildered as I felt. Some were given a similar-looking bag, others just sat on the chairs, chins resting on the backs of their hands. Some had their hands folded in their laps, others were slouched in their seats, completely disengaged. After about fifteen minutes, a man I assumed to be a bus driver emerged from an executive-type coach bus, entered the room and said, "Please find a seat on the bus outside." Fifteen or so of us walked behind the driver in a single file, stepped onto the coach and sat quietly. From there, we drove for over an hour, arriving in a desert of barren land, dried out grass and chalky dry dirt in patches where the grass didn't grow. The doors of the bus opened and three adults starting barking orders at us. Screaming, I mean *SCREAMING* in loud voices. "GET YOUR

LUGGAGE," they shouted, "COME INTO THE HOUSE AND FIND A BEDROOM."

The house was an old 1970s split-level with two short sets of stairs, one running upward and one going down toward a basement area covered with linoleum flooring. The upstairs bedrooms each housed three sets of bunk beds, and no other sleeping options. "Seriously?" I thought to myself. "I'm a grown adult. I haven't shared a bedroom with anyone other than my wife in well over a decade. I paid all this money to come to this old house to share a room with five strangers?" I indignantly voiced to no one. I cursed myself, wondering what had possessed me to sign up for this encounter. I was starting to think that I had followed Ken's recommendation rather blindly; I was starting to remember that Ken and I don't really know each other that well and maybe I had misread the whole situation.

That evening, the over-the-top yelling that had greeted us as we descended the steps of the bus continued. It wasn't that anyone was angry, and it wasn't just the facilitators who were expected to talk like that. All of us were directed to speak in a deafening tone, in an effort, I learned later, to stir feelings of extreme passion. If I tried to talk at a normal speaking volume, one of the leaders would immediately shout, "I CAN'T HEAR YOU! SAY IT AGAIN, AS LOUDLY AS YOU CAN." After dinner, we reconvened and seated ourselves in chairs in a garage that had been converted into a classroom. The yelling persisted. This uncomfortable experience continued until after one in the morning when we were finally dismissed to sleep for a few hours.

The next day seemed to present more of the same. There was a long and exhaustive period of group and individual exercises and lectures. But then, in the afternoon, we were given the task that would change the course of my life. Looking back, I could separate my life into two distinct portions: that which existed before the exercise, and that which has occurred since.

The assignment was: Write the eulogy for your own funeral. We were given twenty minutes to complete this exercise. Once done, we were expected to share our writings with the others, thankfully at a normal volume this time. Without time to be creative or dramatic, I guess you could say my eulogy was pretty standard. It began something like, "Alan was a kind and loving man and an extraordinary husband and father who made obvious the importance of his family. Everyone who knew Alan knew they could count on him as easily for fun as for advice and support. He was a strong leader, both personally and professionally, was an active and giving member of his community. He was deeply committed to what he believed in and never gave up his principles for the sake of comfort." I recall that it ended with, "While Alan is no longer on this earth, his impact will be felt intensely by those of us whose lives he touched."

The facilitators asked me the same simple question they asked to each of the readers as they went around the room: "Could that be said of you today if you were to pass away suddenly?" While we all had different versions of eulogies, the question was answered again and again, by each participant, in the same way. Simply, "No."

By then, I don't think I was the only one who was exhausted by the intensity of emotion we had been pushed to explore over the last twenty-eight hours. Like the others, I was broken down by the demand to look the reality of our lives squarely in the face. After we had shared our eulogies, we were assigned to write a vision statement that would begin to close the gap between the life we were currently living and the life we wanted to be living. As darkness descended outside, in that old garage room, amidst a group of strangers, tired and raw, I took pen to paper. Right there and then, the **5 Fs** were born.

FAMILY

FAITH

FITNESS

FORTUNE

FUN/FRIENDS

Chapter 5
Beyond Creating the Vision

Knowing that I'd never be accountable to a mission statement I couldn't remember the words of, I was pleased that I had been able to categorize my life goals into five key areas. I knew, however, that it was one thing to name what needed to be done, and another thing altogether to actually do the work.

I remember leaving the training utterly exhausted but hopeful in a way I had glimpsed months earlier when talking to Ken. My wife must have sensed that I was returning from a life-altering experience; she and the kids were unexpectedly waiting at the airport when I landed Sunday evening from Nevada. Completely out of character, I found myself crying as I hugged my family.

Over the next several weeks, I set about trying to understand why each of the **5 F's** had leapt onto my paper. Knowing the real work was about to begin, I spent time writing down at least one way I could make a small improvement in each of the five areas. I knew about goals and I knew I knew how to achieve them. Afterall, being a competitive swimmer taught me the importance of having goals. Now, fifteen years after getting out of the pool, I believed I could use all that I had learned through the sport to "fix" myself.

Knowing that I had taken the first step of identifying where work could be done, I felt revitalized. I now had distinct areas in which to focus my energy, rather than an overwhelming chaotic mess that needed resolution but had no clear boundaries. Identifying the problem has always been the first step when I approach anything, and so, for the first time since facing the tangle that was my life, I felt confident that one step would lead to the next. I knew that being able to celebrate each small step along the way would keep me motivated and focused.

How I maintained that motivation and focus over these past almost twenty years, and how it brought me deeper fulfillment than I ever imagined possible, is the content of the following chapters.

Part II

Chapter 6
The Journey

I have shared my childhood struggles; I have described how I became deeply driven to satisfy myself and myself alone. I've illustrated my race to have a "perfect life", and then described how I saw my life quake under my feet. Luckily, I had an experience of awareness that helped me understand how to turn my life around. I am writing this book, sharing so openly my experiences, because I know I'm not the only one who faces intense challenges in a modern world of competing priorities. I know that many who have been driven to great success in business have struggled to also have a healthy home life, a healthy body, or a healthy ability to rest and enjoy life. Without the help of others like Ken and the facilitators of that fateful Empowerment training, I likely would have lost my family and perhaps my health, living a life I hoped I never had to live. And so, because I was helped at just the moment when I needed it most, I want to offer the same lifeline to anyone who might need it. I want to say to you: you too can make impactful changes in your life; you just need to take one step at a time.

It's all about naming the priorities in your life. It's all about finding out first what matters most to you. What matters today, and as importantly, what will matter years from now when you are looking at your life, lived in the rearview mirror? What will give you a sense of peace and fulfilment? These are the questions I faced when I wrote my vision statement.

For the remainder of the book, I'll explain how I apply each of the **5 Fs** specifically, but also more generally so that you are able to apply them to your own life. I have taken the liberty of expanding the definition of each so that they are broad enough to apply to all kinds of people with all different experiences. I ask that you keep an open mind about the meanings as well. I don't take ownership over these ideals; rather, they seemed to come through me that day when I was completely desperate, by some act of grace that decided to save me from myself. In this vein, I offer them to you.

Please know that adopting these principles is not a silver bullet that will take you straight to complete life fulfilment. It's a journey you have to commit to, over and over again, every day of your life. Time and again, I come back the **5 Fs**, reviewing each individually, and also collectively in order to find balance in my life. It helps to remember these stories I am about to share with you, so that I can remember why these things are important to me. I hope you will find inspiration in them too.

Chapter 7
FAMILY

Intuitively, I knew that my family was important to me. What I didn't know and only learned through many years and literally dozens of trying situations, was that the time and attention required to nurture this part of my life doesn't come as easily to me as I wish it did. I am struck over and over by the example that was shared during that fateful leadership training. "Imagine you pull into the driveway after a long day at work," the facilitator had said. "Your kids are playing with an insect in the driveway and excitedly call out to you to come see what they've caught. You're too exhausted to be bothered and instead walk right by, saying you'll look at it later. In that moment, you shattered your child." This lesson struck a nerve and although I sat there in class trying to rationalize similar behaviors of mine that came to mind, trying to claim that my kids were fine with my dismissive responses, I knew I was guilty of this conduct. Although it seems hard to believe after all these years, I think it was honestly the first time that I had any inkling of just some of the shortcomings that Jill had been describing. I realized that rather than feeling irritated with Jill, I should be grateful for her concerns. In reality, she was trying to save me from myself. Although I had been honoring "four o'clock Fridays" for many months, I was doing so because I had made a promise to Jill. When the example during the Empowerment experience made me realize how emotionally unavailable I was, I vowed to take responsibility for my actions, and set about preparing steps to fulfill this promise. Luckily, the boys were still young. At the top of the list was my pledge to attend activities for my boys' events such as baseball games and swim meets. I started with one a week, building up to attending every single event if I was in town. Next, I started to turn off the TV instead of tuning out in front of it, so that I could play catch with my sons. I knew I was beginning to make some progress towards being a better father. I still had a long road ahead, but the small steps were a great start, and I continued making other similar small steps as my boys grew.

When my sons got older, the dynamics shifted, and I realized that doing things only as a family was no longer enough. I needed to build my own relationship with each of my sons or I would lose them to the worlds in which they lived. I began to make sure I was home for dinners when my sons' friends and various girlfriends were guests, instead of only hearing about the visits from my wife. And when the boys went to college, I knew it wasn't enough to hear about their lives through Jill's phone conversations; I too had to make my own calls.

These small steps over the years led the way toward a not-so-small change in myself. But I was about to be tested in a way I had never before experienced. Luckily, the accumulation of the small changes, the small commitments made over the years made me strong enough to take the next big step: that of real emotional growth.

Jill's diagnosis came after a routine mammogram. When something suspicious was found on the mammogram, a stereotactic biopsy was performed. Not one to be overly alarmed, Jill had told me I didn't need to go with her to the doctor on the day of the biopsy. Something however nagged at the edge of my conscience, and I surprised her by showing up not only at that appointment, but also at the follow-up doctor's appointment when she was getting the results. As soon as we heard the words "malignant tumor" followed by the doctor's comment, "We need to talk about options," I went into planning mode. After all, I'd been training myself my whole life: lay out a plan and execute. It's what I mastered professionally every day. Jill on the other hand, was shocked and confused; she couldn't decipher the options and asked me to make the decision about treatment. This was a Tuesday; on Friday, she underwent a lumpectomy, followed by thirty-three radiation treatments over six weeks. During these weeks of radiation, Jill lived with her mom. We had recently sold our home and the one we were building was not quite ready.

We were treading uncharted territory, having never dealt with a health problem like this before. By this point, I had worked with the **5 Fs** for eighteen years, and I knew that the first thing I needed to do was to take a step back and evaluate how I was doing in the balance of my life. Observing myself, I noticed that I was keeping myself busy, keeping up with Jill's treatments as if she were a project in the category of Finance, instead of my wife. I even knew that I was doing this so that I didn't have to feel afraid or to grieve the situation. I was grateful that Jill was living with her mom who nurtured her and cared for her by preparing well balanced meals every day and allowing her to rest a lot. Seeing all this for what it was, it was clear that there was imbalance, and that the Family **F** needed to be squarely repositioned front and center in my life. During this period, I was working in town, almost two hours away from Jill's mom, but I intuitively knew the importance of being with Jill as often as possible. I started to attend as many Friday radiation sessions that I could. I tried to lighten her spirits by talking with her throughout each treatment that I was able to attend. Needing to allow herself to be taken care of, I recognized that Jill was in a vulnerable position; I found that I had grown enough to know how to be emotionally available to Jill.

I don't believe that Jill was ever at a high risk of dying from her cancer, but it was on the spectrum of a disease that took lives every day. Early on when Jill asked for a divorce, although she was completely serious about what she was saying, I sensed that there was still a small chance that I could make the changes that would convince her to allow me to stay. The cancer was a different threat. There was nothing I could do or change to make her cancer better; it was out of my hands. Knowing that I was unable to control a disease that could ravage my wife's body scared me. It humbled me. Now, I didn't have to be following my step-by-step plan to know that I should show up for family instead of going to one more business meeting. Now, that business meeting became completely irrelevant. Rescheduling a dinner with my boss no longer took a force of will. All of this was happening on its own, out of my own desires.

Still, it wasn't until months later, during National Breast Cancer Awareness month, that the reality of Jill's illness finally hit me. By then, I realized, my wife was a "cancer survivor." What if she hadn't survived? It hit me how much I needed Jill, how scared I was to lose her, and how essential my family really is to me. I had come a long way since that leadership training nearly eighteen years earlier. I felt extremely satisfied that I was able to evaluate my values and make changes in my actions that made me more available for contributions to Jill's treatment. I would soon learn however that my family was not done becoming important to me.

Within six months of Jill's final treatment, I faced another challenge that would require another huge climb toward emotional growth. As part of a reorganization at work, we had recently had an assessment of how we were performing in our positions. The company needed to change its model, and cutbacks were a key component. Said a different way, the restructure would impact a group of people; I would be one of them. At this point, I had been there for thirty years, and had survived over a dozen such changes. My boss put a meeting on my calendar for the Friday before the new organization was to be announced. Entering my boss's office early that day, I'll never forget the bluntness of his words: "The purpose of our conversation this morning is to inform you of the results of the assessment. You fell below the line and your last day with the company will be three months from now, February 28th. Please ensure a smooth transition to your replacement and then you don't need to come in again." All this before I sat down. I took a seat, looked at him and said, "Good Morning." And then I got up and left.

Shortly after the meeting, I began to process that I had failed; stunned, I went home. Unable to make sense of everything that had happened, feeling sick, I went to bed. I did nothing all weekend. On Monday, I returned to the office, where I completed some deadline-driven work. By Wednesday afternoon, I was tired of the line of people waiting outside my office to give me their sympathy. Part of my transition was to close out the year and pass on critical knowledge to my successor. This time turned out to be another dark period of my life, both physically and emotionally. Everything I had learned and practiced over the eighteen years since I wrote my personal mission statement fled my mind as my body was overcome by the physical stress and anxiety over which I was out of control.

What began as a winter cold on that Wednesday turned into what felt like the flu by Friday, and I rested all weekend, feeling a little better by Monday. I met with colleagues that I considered to be true friends, and, warmed by their outrage and disbelief of my job loss, I clung to the notion that I was being treated unfairly. The pressure was too much, though, and I found myself back in bed by Thursday of the next week. I went to bed at six that evening and did not wake up until Saturday morning. As I got out of bed, I collapsed to the floor. Minutes later, I found myself in an uncontrollable sweat, completely light-headed, and filled with an angst that manifested in very shallow breaths. I did not know what was happening, but believed I was having a heart attack or stroke. I knew something was not right. I got up and immediately went to the hospital. When an assembly of nurses swarmed the hospital room, a heart monitor uncovered a moderate case of arrhythmia, and fluid around my heart revealed congestive heart failure. What transpired over the next several weeks felt like scenes from a television show. There was an ambulance, IV drips, paddles for electrical cardioversion treatments, pills, talks of blood clots, and possible stroke. My family came in and out of the ICU, the pastor from my mother-in-law's church prayed over me. Almost two decades earlier, at the leadership experience, I was asked to fake my eulogy; that week I was literally planning my funeral, down to the last detail. I was out of control, unprepared and had no ability to plan next steps and execute. Unlike during Jill's illness, where she had months to deal and I had months to plan, the time I had felt like minutes remaining. It was then that I had my first and only verbal conversation with God.

I prayed out loud for the first time in my life. And what I found myself praying about was my family. I again realized that they were what mattered first and last in life. My family was my lifeline; I needed them, I loved them, I needed to know they would be taken care of. In that moment, connected by a fragile thread to life, my work never even entered my mind. I cared only about whether I had been the kind of husband and father I wanted to be. There was no check list I referenced, there was nothing other than listening to the words of my heart. I knew in that moment, that while not perfect, I was significantly closer to the kind of man I wanted to be than I was when I first wrote my eulogy more than eighteen years before. Because I had taken one step at a time, I was able to cover more ground than I would have thought possible as I marched toward what mattered in my life.

***

Perhaps you too have had experiences that led to a similar roller-coaster ride of emotion. Whether you feel fulfilled in your personal relationships, feel complete emptiness, or most likely feel something in between, I encourage you to take the time to consider the people in your life that matter the most. Today, family can appear in so many different sizes and shapes. Think beyond the traditional definition of family if the traditional one doesn't work for you. Family may refer to your biological or blood family, but for many people, family includes people you *choose*. Family are the people that make your life better simply because they are a part of it. Looking at this aspect of your life can be very painful, as it was for me. In my adulthood, I had to realize that I wasn't showing up for my family in the way that I deeply needed. Sometimes we take for granted, or even push away the people we value the most. I urge you to take courage and ask yourself whether you are really showing up for those you love. You can change your life right now by taking small steps to become the partner, parent, friend, sibling that you want to be. Start by listing the people that matter to you, and then write down two to three things that really matter to *them*. Next to each one of those things, consider a way you can participate in that part of their life. Remember that small steps lead the way to big changes.

FAMILY: *Use this section to identify those people that matter most. Identify their needs and why it matters if you honor their values. Brainstorm on how you can engage. Or, use the space to understand what family means to you and how you can be in a fulfilling relationship.*

Why is it important to me to honor the people I love by acknowledging and engaging in their values?

_____
_____
_____

1. Who matters? _____

What matters to this person?

_____
_____
_____

How can I engage?

_____
_____
_____
_____

2. Who matters? _____

What matters to this person?

_____
_____
_____
_____

How can I engage?

_____
_____
_____
_____

3. Who matters? _____

What matters to this person?

_____
_____
_____
_____

How can I engage?

_____
_____
_____
_____

Chapter 8
FAITH

Religion came back into my life in small, seemingly unconnected ways that, in aggregate, could no longer be ignored.

After I returned from the Empowerment session, the constant hum of faith was present in the background of my mind. I knew that it was something of deep importance to me, though it had been latent for a long time. Why else would it have surfaced as one of my five values?

My religion had once been a huge part of my life. I didn't question this. Between the ages of nine and twenty-one, I went to church every Sunday. In my mid-teens, I was confirmed in the Methodist Church. Proactively, I was my college's student body representative for the Methodists on campus. I taught Sunday school and belonged to the fellowship for Christian Athletes.

However, by the time I was graduating from college, I found myself questioning what it meant to believe, as so many young people do. I saw people wearing crosses, but instead of feeling a connection to that holy symbol, I felt nothing. A kind of emptiness took over where unquestioning faith had been. I began to fill that space with other things.

Rather unconsciously, I started to abandon the structured religious engagements of my upbringings. I simply stopped going to church after I got married, and other activities on my calendar began to take precedence.

Not long after our oldest was born, I remember googling the word "faith." I can no longer recall the impetus for the search, but I remember reading the definition, "complete trust or confidence in someone or something," and feeling wholly disconnected from the concept. The words "spiritual apprehension rather than proof" sounded good, in theory, but I had no idea what "spiritual apprehension" might mean, and I suppose I didn't care. I thought no more about it for the next several years.

But something happened to me around this disconnection from faith when I wrote the eulogy for myself years ago during the leadership training. After rereading my words, I realized that I did not mention God or my faith at all. The absence of any reference to God felt like just that: an absence. I wondered if something was missing. Did I miss God?

I realized that as a child, I was taught not to question, but rather to simply believe, to have faith in my religion. As a young adult learning about the world, I saw how people followed faith without question, and I didn't like it. So, I rejected all of it, pushing it away from myself and completely ignoring the question altogether. I rejected without question.

As I grew older, and around the time of my participation at Empowerment, I was having a nagging feeling that told me that full rejection wasn't quite right either. I didn't have to go in for blind faith, but perhaps there was a faith I felt to be a true part of myself, one that was "spiritually apprehended." Though I vaguely sensed my need for this, I was still at a loss as to how to reunite with that part of myself.

One Sunday, not too long after I returned home from my weekend leadership training, I found myself alone as Jill and the boys were out of town with her family. Without any forethought, I decided to go to church. I hadn't planned it but awoke with such an intense conviction that I needed to go to church, that I knew the time was right. Perhaps it was the fact that I didn't need to explain to anyone why I wanted to go, perhaps it was knowing that I could absorb the service without discussion or explanation, but, whatever the reason, I heard the call and I went. I went in search of answers.

Sitting in the pew as sounds of beautiful verse filled the room, a great familiarity tugged at a place deep in my chest. A lot of time had passed since my last visit to church, but the feeling was recognizable. I wanted to lose myself in that feeling and not allow my doubts to interfere. However, a deeper memory of earlier days troubled my peace, and I knew attending this worship service had somehow complicated my life. I knew I would have to face the questions that surfaced.

I took as a good omen the fact that the pastor of the service had the same alma mater as I. The shared background made accessible to me, this otherwise intimidating person. Still, it was with trepidation that I would visit with the Pastor regularly. I asked him my questions. We talked about my upbringing, the mixed feelings I had about allowing religion to enter my life, the things I couldn't believe in. When I found myself completely overwhelmed by the unknown, the pastor would say, simply, "Trust me." As time passed, and the sessions grew in number, I found that I did trust him. What became clear to me was that I could pick and choose what felt relevant and meaningful to me, without being torn by the contradictions of this way of thinking.

If church was going to be a part of my life, I knew I needed my family to participate. We all attended services and other events together. And so, we began to attend church services weekly, monthly church dinners, and later even attending bible study classes. Feeling more and more comfortable with my relationship to faith, I found that my religion had begun to bring the richness to my spiritual life that had been missing all those years.

Once I had opened myself up to the journey back to faith and religion, faith came resolutely knocking on my door in one very surprising and uncanny way. Retreating to the workshop in the basement of my house one Saturday afternoon, I had happily busied myself with building a wood frame for a new painting my wife had completed. As I worked, I was surrounded by awards and other keepsakes that hung on the wall, a collection of memories too dear to trash but not recent or significant enough to have a place in the main part of the house. One of these mementoes was a plaque displaying my name as the recipient of a local memorial award, which was given annually in the memory of a young girl who drowned while swimming at our community pool. Her family sponsored this award, a scholarship in the girl's name that was given to a high school senior who exemplified sportsmanship, dedication, effort, team spirit and inspiration. This award, like the others displayed, was a permanent fixture on the wall. The collection had become like wallpaper to me: existing as a backdrop to my projects, unmemorable.

On this Saturday, I was using a nail gun to hammer the edges of the frame together, when the sheer force caused that award to fall off the wall, dislodging the front plate of the plaque. Not thinking much about it, I picked it off the floor, and laid it on top of my workbench to repair later.

To further explain how coincidental the timing was, it's important to know that the girl that drowned had had two brothers that were slightly older than me. I hadn't really been especially close to either of them, and I hadn't seen them or even heard anything about them in well over twenty-five years. I wasn't even in contact with anyone who knew them. They were a part of my distant past, insignificant in my life. That evening, though, when I logged in to check my emails before going to bed, at the top of my inbox was an email from one of the brothers. I opened it. He had written to invite me to attend a service at the local Masonic Lodge. The coincidence was too stunning to resist. I emailed him back.

My personal journey through the Masonic Lodge further changed me. Although I have no intention of proselytizing for this sect of religion, for me, it worked. The fact that there are no priests nor ministers nor rabbis rang true to me. Having no system of clergy means that everybody is their own thinker. Strangely, although we don't worship any particular doctrine, we do share an acknowledgement of something greater than ourselves. A higher power is central in our lives, compelling us to do good in our community; this altruism is the only required commonality. We take these obligations seriously, and we believe that if we don't believe in something bigger than ourselves, the obligation means nothing.

For me personally, this means that my faith is about being a good person. The sacred places and rituals that were so regimented in my early years, and then so confusing in my adult life have been replaced by the sacredness of goodness and decency amongst people.

Deeply seeded in my upbringing, perhaps the Faith **F** is the most traveled journey of all. Present in so many different forms throughout my life, I realize that it created sometimes the most confusion but also the most clarity. In many ways, it sits at the core of all that I value.

Traveling the winding path I did, with all the places of doubt and rejection, it means a lot to me that over the years, my journey has allowed me to connect enough to my faith that I stood in the place of honor when I was asked to officiate my son's wedding!

***

Today, I am convinced that faith means different things to different people at different times in their lives. The journey that I traveled was both confusing and comforting throughout my life. Take some time to understand what it is you have faith in, and what does that mean for your life. What exists outside yourself that drives you to be the kind of person you want to be?   It could be a higher power, it could be science, kindness or even love. How does it enter into the choices you make every day? It's one thing to say you have faith in something and another altogether to put it into practice. The reason it is one of my five **Fs** is that it takes a lot of intentionality to maintain the balance in this area of my life. This is a somewhat silent **F** since it doesn't have a material presence. But when we neglect it, something inside of us suffers.

FAITH: *Use this section to understand your needs and beliefs around faith. Below are thought-starter questions. Answer these, or other questions tugging at your mind.*

Faith can be different than religion. What do you have faith in?

_____
_____
_____
_____

What does your faith mean to you?

_____
_____
_____
_____
_____

What does your faith impact in your life? And the choices you make?

_____
_____
_____
_____
_____

How can you incorporate whatever you believe in into your everyday life?

_____
_____
_____
_____

Can you think of a time when you didn't have faith and how it impacted you?

_____
_____
_____
_____

Chapter 9

FITNESS

One of the most significant lessons I learned from the Fitness **F** is that things can get out of balance, not only by not doing enough in an area, but equally as detrimental, by doing too much.

Early on, swimming comforted me. The very act became a way to disconnect from everything that created tension and stress in my life. Through swimming, I also learned to rely on myself and to succeed for only me. While these early lessons are now eye-opening about the harsh realities of my childhood, at the time they amounted to a feeling of pure pleasure of the sport. I recently found a series of papers in the form of a questionnaire I had completed when I was thirteen and then completed again two years later. Under the "five things I value most in life" section on both lists was "swimming". Although by the age of fifteen, I had tempered my dream list from "winning a gold medal in the Olympics," written when I was thirteen, to simply "make it to the Olympics," clearly this sport was a key component in my life.

But I wasn't thinking about fitness, in the sense of keeping my body healthy, when I started swimming. I just loved it. Like most kids, my metabolism was fast; I could eat whatever I wanted without gaining weight or otherwise suffering. Once, after a physical exam, my doctor told me that, because I was in such good physical shape, my body would demand that I exercise the rest of my life. It was at that moment that physical activity became not only a pleasure but also a job to me. Even as a teen, anything with specific goals, definite rules and exact roadmaps made me feel secure. I did not shy away from this job.

I do admit, however, that my physical activity waned for periods of time during my adult life, particularly when I was building my career and working seventy-hour weeks. In retrospect, I see myself coming back to it time and again, seeking this outlet when time permitted. In the early years of our marriage, Jill and I took long walks and hikes, and we biked and played tennis on occasion. Later, I golfed with my boys, went on camping trips and played ball in the yard. Although these were intermittent, they were present enough to help me realize that keeping physically active was important. When I went too long without movement, I started to feel sluggish.

When I built my vision, although Fitness clearly made my top five list, I did not believe it was an area in which I needed much work. I felt immensely grateful for this gift since the other 4 **Fs** required so much time! It came as a huge surprise when I realized that I really hadn't nailed this **F**. My first revelation came not at once but through a sequence of competitions over the previous five-year period. It began with running a series of 10K races, and then I graduated to mini triathlons. Next, I decided to challenge myself by competing in the 1.25-mile swim from Alcatraz to Aquatic Park in San Francisco Bay. I hadn't swum in years, so, like I did with everything, I set small goals to lead me to the big one. I established a training routine, hired a personal trainer, lifted weights and even set up practice swims off boats at Lake Lanier, a local lake near my home. As I got my body back in shape, shedding pounds and gaining strength, I felt physically fantastic. I was ready for the race, and I proudly completed it under the time I had set for myself. I celebrated the win by sharing with others my accomplishment and deep satisfaction. The small letdown that I felt, the one that came after the completion of every race, simply meant that I would have to sign up for another. With the next goal in front of me, I pushed on. More remnants perhaps from my early childhood when being good was "never good enough."

You can probably see how my training became an obsession. With each accomplished event, I wanted to complete another, more challenging and more difficult. And then, it wasn't enough to simply participate in these competitive challenges; I was driven to finish in the top among my age group. I started taking time away from my family, getting off balance in the life I had strived so hard to stabilize.

Six years ago, I trained for my first and only half IRONMAN. This triathlon consists of a 1.2-mile swim, a 56-mile bicycle ride and a 13.1-mile run, raced in that order, without a break. There is a limit on completion time, and I successfully completed the race under that time.

The preparation for a race of this intensity is no small task. It cannot be done without tilting the rest of life out of balance, and I started taking time away from my family and the other important areas of my life. When the race ended, and the goal was satisfied, I was literally traumatized by the complete emotional and physical let-down that came afterwards. With the other **Fs** so starved for attention, I was left without any way to nourish my soul. Rather than marveling at my capability, I felt empty and confused. Even now, years later, I still haven't been able to process this aimlessness. I still have not gotten over this disappointment, and I find myself wondering how I could be so wrong about what would satisfy and fulfill me.

Trying to heal my letdown, I began to see the similarities between how I trained for an extreme sport and how I worked obsessively in the early years of my career. I realized that my tendency towards extremes was neither healthy nor good for me. Focusing on one **F** at the detriment of the others consumes too much time and zaps too much energy. How can I be the kind of man I want to be if I allow myself to be so self-focused?

With this inkling that winning awards was not more important than balancing all that mattered in my life, I learned another key lesson about fitness when my wife's health was challenged. Although I would train intensively over a period of time, the existence of these periods of training did not cancel out or make up for the other times when I abused my body. During those times, I made unhealthy choices - you know the kind - which had a way of creeping up and culminating in feeling lethargic and lazy. It was time for me to understand that fitness of body had to do, not only with working out, but also with what I put into my body, and about how critical it was that I do a better job of prioritizing sleep.

Focusing on our new definition of fitness, I went about implementing a healthier regimen. Although difficult at first, the physical gains that kicked in almost immediately made me feel a lot better and feeling good helped me stay on track. I found that setting small goals to eliminate the unhealthy choices allowed me to get my eating and drinking under control. I minimized alcohol, then sweets, then bread and so on until I was eating all the right foods. I eliminated caffeine. Once accomplished, I allowed myself to get back to the philosophy of "everything in moderation." Now, I allow myself a glass of wine with dinner a few nights a week, a cocktail on the weekend, a dessert on occasion. Although I do slip up on more than I'd like to, in general I am eating well and exercising regularly, all of which allows me to sleep peacefully at night.

***

Even if we all agree that exercise and healthy food and drink choices are important to our overall health, because each person's body is different, it is important to determine what fitness looks like and feels like to *you* personally. Be true to yourself and honestly assess your true needs, even if you know there will be inherent challenges in reaching them. With the Fitness **F** in particular, you can take small goals to improve your overall fitness. One leads to the next in perhaps a more linear fashion than with some of the other **Fs**. However, this is an area where we might slide backwards more than we want to. Be careful to set goals that are attainable and sustainable, knowing that there are likely to be starts and stops. That is okay. You should forgive yourself for the small transgressions, knowing you even moving forward a little at a time is helpful. There are numerous books and philosophies about how to achieve better fitness because there is no one way to approach maintaining a healthy lifestyle. It's about what works for you. What does it mean to eat in a healthy way, to drink in moderation? How much sleep do you need? And what does it mean to you to be physically fit? Finally, are you taking the other **Fs** into account as you balance this one? It is always important to come back to balance. Remember to celebrate the wins as they are achieved before moving on to the next goal. Work the steps to gain the strides.

Fitness: Use this section to jot down thoughts around fitness. Below are thought-starter questions. Answer these, or other questions that feel more relevant.

What does fitness mean to you? Is it about exercise, eating/drinking habits, sleep, something else?

_____
_____
_____
_____
_____

Are you achieving your desired level of nutrition? If not, why not?

_____
_____
_____
_____

Is maintaining an active lifestyle important to you?

_____
_____
_____
_____

What steps can you take to get to a higher level of fitness?

_____
_____
_____
_____
_____

How much sleep do you need? Are you getting it? If not, what can you do to change that?

_____
_____
_____
_____
_____

Chapter 10
FORTUNE

Someone asked me recently if I had the chance to rewrite my career path, would I go about it in the same way? My gut reaction was to say no, but after really thinking about it, I know that my answer was only partially true. In reality, I lived and learned more than I ever dared to expect. But the cost was high, the toll large, and that reality is what caused my instant response.

Yet, I know that I would be much different today if I didn't face the trials, the disappointments, the stress . . . but also the wins and the triumphs that I did. On the simplest level, if I could go back though and do it all again, I would do it differently. I would slow down my trajectory, not be in such a rush, learn to be more satisfied with the accomplishments along the way. I would focus more on my outside interests, spend more time with mentors, ask more questions. I would pay more attention to my health and especially be more available to my family. Yet, hindsight is glaringly bright. Although I would have liked to have done things differently, I'm certain that I would not have learned what really matters most to me if I had done things differently. And so, in this vein, I would not sacrifice either the pain or the accomplishments to learn all that I did.

Among the key lessons I learned is that fortune is about so much more than money. In truth, I had always given lip-service to this notion, but the older I get, the more I ascribe to this adage. On a professional level, I've always believed that being successful in a career is of great value. What I've learned recently is that the amount of the paycheck doesn't define the value. To me, fortune is about being in a leadership position where others look to me for mentorship, compassion, decision making and direction. I adamantly believe that there is no magic level that every person should strive to reach in a career, there is no set amount of money that must be in the bank or in a portfolio to define success. As it should, success in a career means something different to each of us. I have worked with really happy and quite successful people who didn't want to advance beyond a certain point in their career; they were high achievers and strong performers who were comfortable in their position. And happy. I also know people who worry less about their bank balance or their material possessions. There are those who work for something altogether different from a career, and still "fortune" is about being successful in whatever they consider their purpose. There is a part of me that envies those who learned this lesson sooner than I.

This **F** is the most difficult for me, because it is so easy for me to get out of balance. I am continually in some level of internal conflict between my inclination to strive for more career success and money, and my emotional self that has been slowly awakened through the years in recognition of other needs and desires in my life.

Understanding how to incorporate the Fortune **F** meant that I had to find a way to change the way I worked and still achieve the career success and the financial level I wanted. In my career, I introduced new concepts of efficiency and effectiveness in my workplace, and while I constantly pushed for better systems and processes to create this productivity, I wasn't able to extend this philosophy to the way I personally went to work. I could identify ways for my group to work smarter, but I didn't apply these same rules to my personal style. My thinking was skewed: even if I could accomplish what needed to be done in forty or fifty hours a week, I felt as if I needed to be at work seventy or more hours each week. Although earning a raise of 2-3% a year would have allowed me to reach my goals, I still strived for the 5-6% range. In the beginning of my work with the **5 Fs**, when I went walking along the executive floors in our building, I noticed that, while I knew what everyone's job was, I knew absolutely nothing about their personal lives, what they cared about, what they liked to do for fun, whether they had families. This way of living did not support the kind of man I wanted to be.

I knew I needed to change something. To reduce my 70-80-hour weeks, I decided on an experiment during which I worked only eight hours a day for ten days. By my own rules, I wasn't allowed to bring home my computer and I couldn't respond to any beeper calls (yes, it was that long ago!) At the beginning of each day, I set my daily goals, tasks and to-do lists. At the end of the day, I checked off what I had accomplished, reviewed the items left undone, and compiled the next day's list. On the eleventh day, looking for common themes, I developed three rules by which to guide my work life.

1) **Make sure that the value I am bringing to a meeting is clear to me.** If I don't know what my contribution is, I probably don't need to be at that meeting.

2) **Take time to determine whether a meeting is really necessary.** Sometimes what I call a "drive by" is good enough. This could be a coffee with someone or even walking to a meeting with someone to focus on an issue. Shorter touch points are the goal.

3) **Spend more time with people on people.** What makes my friend Ken so great at his job is that he spends eighty percent of his time with people. Skills to run financial analyses can be taught,

tweaked and raised up a notch or two when necessary. But connecting with people, learning who they are keeps them engaged and makes the workplace a happier and healthier place to be for all of us. People feel appreciated for their contributions.

The shift to these three simple rules carried me through the next dozen or more years of my career, and I worked hard at following these important principles. I opted out of meetings more frequently, I communicated and got together with others in shorter, more sociable and creative venues. I tried to understand on an individual basis what motivates people, how they like to receive recognition, and some of their outside interests. I found I was happier, and, amazingly, I started to like myself better. However, I was still finding it difficult to grow into my leadership role and remain humble, so I knew I still had a lot of learning and growing to do.

I realized less than one year ago, right after I had my health scare, that when I leave my career of thirty plus years, I will be taking little with me. As previously stated, I have some regrets that I did not do things differently. Sure, I reached my retirement goals, and I have the numerous skills I learned and honed over the years, and while I am incredibly grateful for these, they are not enough to take with me. A mentor recently told me that being successful at our company was about forming networks both horizontally and vertically in the building. He was saying that being successful here meant all my energies were spent on being relevant to those higher up and on peers, leaving little time or room for those outside of this company or those within the company who would not benefit me professionally. What I regret is that I did not focus more on the relationships, and the friendships I could take with me.

With retirement now knocking at my door, striving for fortune looks and feels different. Clearly, the end is a bittersweet reality of mixed emotions. At the time of this writing, I have just learned that I was voted one of the top 100 people in finance for 2019 by Top 100 Magazine. This publication is distributed to all fifty states and over a hundred countries - this humbles me. I am flattered, and I also know that the credit does not belong to me alone. It belongs to all those people who tirelessly worked for me and with me. It belongs to the mentors I had along the way. And it belongs to my family who stuck by me as I focused on the career success I desired. I thought the awards and recognition would be the most important marker of all. How wrong I was. The legacy that matters most is that I have made a difference to people with whom I've worked and lived. I think often about the Warner Bros 1994 Richie Rich movie during which the robbers attempt to open the secured vault in search of hidden treasures. What they find when the safe is finally opened are a multitude of memories and other keepsakes. They are disappointed. I know however that these are the true treasures in life.

Today I think of my retirement from my corporate job as more of a career shift. There are so many classes I put on hold, so many technical skills as well as topics of interest I want to continue learning. With all the unknowns, I am certain that there are many opportunities and jobs I never even considered. From a professional perspective, I know that I'm not ready to retire. I still have some work years left in me. I know that I still want to set an alarm, be accountable to be somewhere, and have goals to meet. With chasing passions instead of pinnacles as my new mission, I'm able to take the lessons I've learned and seek new opportunities, spread my wings so to speak in a in a way I never have before. The future of possibilities feels like a balanced way to keep up with the **F** that represents Fortune.

***

The lessons I learned around Fortune are probably the clearest to my readers out of any of these chapters. The success driven mentality might describe you or someone you know. On the one hand, that drive got me to where I am, and perhaps it's what led you, the reader, to find out who I am or to pick up this book. It is my hope that sharing my experience might help you understand earlier than I did what it is that drives you to success. What does fortune look like and is there an easier path to travel that will give you the satisfaction you need? Fortune is something that should be revisited and evaluated with an open mind as you go through your life. Allow it to change as you grow and understand your true needs. As I illustrated in the first part of this book, the success came at a great cost and I've had to learn many lessons in order to bring true value and meaning beyond financial success back into my life. And it worked. It is totally possible to find that balance. It's something you have to work at every day; it is just one area that needs balance.

Fortune: *Use this section to sort through your values with respect to fortune. Below are thought-starter questions. Answer these, or other questions that feel more relevant.*

Who do you think has amassed great fortune? Why?

_____
_____
_____
_____

How do you define fortune?

_____
_____
_____
_____

What habits or skills are the most important to help you reach that fortune?

_____
_____
_____
_____

What advice would you give to your twenty-year- old self about amassing fortune?

_____

_____
_____
_____

What obstacles are there to achieving your fortune? And how can you mitigate those obstacles?

_____
_____
_____
_____

Chapter 11
FUN/FRIENDS

At the other end of the comfort zone, we arrive at the final **F**, Fun/Friends. This is the one that I am currently striving to embrace the most, and the one with which I have the least experience. I recently was sharing my **5 Fs** with someone who inadvertently substituted "Friends" for "Fun", and I began to realize the connection at this point in my life. Quite honestly, I'm surprised that eighteen years ago I was even able to identify that Fun was even important. It wasn't exactly that I intentionally avoided either friends or fun; I just never realized that I was missing anything.

Early in my life, swimming, with its structured goals and rules was something I liked to do, so in this sense it was fun. Although I was part of a team, swimming is not really a team sport, and I never developed the kinds of friendships that often bind people together in search of a common goal. I never needed anyone else to have fun with while I swam. Sure, I had a buddy or two that I talked to during swim practice or even sat with in classes, but no one that earned a "best friend" title.

After marrying Jill, fun came in the form of family vacations, cruises, Disney World, jet skis, boating, golfing. But fun also came in the form of working on home improvement projects, building things, learning to fly a drone. I remember a driving trip Jill and I took with the kids. We followed a very precise spreadsheet, complete with mile markers and places to stop. Maybe the details of such a trip would be off-putting to someone else, but I look back on that trip and others like it and I think: you know what, that's my kind of fun!

Yes, I know how to have fun in my own way, but I still have not fully mastered the ability to relax with others and have unbridled fun, to simply enjoy spending time together. To be honest, I'm mostly content as a loner, but with more free time available, I'd like to develop more friendships. I admit though, when asked, "What is a friend?" I can't really answer the question. Sure, my wife is my best friend, but marriage by nature, exists in a category all its own. I suppose my early upbringing made me uncomfortable about trusting others, and the lasting effects on my adult life are something I'm working to overcome. I always believed that people wanted something from me if they wanted to be a friend. As a child, I never gained the confidence that people would want to be with me just because they liked me or because I was fun to be around. I learned instead how to be alone.

Because I have spent so much of my adult life at work, it should follow that I have a slew of friends with whom I work. And while close to one hundred people reached out to me when my professional role was impacted, my close friends are only a handful of people that I will continue to see. I say this not to diminish the gifts that I've received from all of the small and large interactions that I had with all who crossed my path, but only to acknowledge that my group of friends is relatively small, and that has always worked for me.

Today, I'm at a true crossroads in my life, and I know that a period of growth and change is around the corner. I've spent the past nearly two decades raising awareness of the important values in my life, working towards being a good husband, a present Dad, a successful businessman. My childhood is long behind me, my kids are grown, and I have closed a chapter on my career. I believe now is the time for the **F** of Fun and Friends to become front and center. Who would've guessed!

I don't know much about it, and I'll admit I'm a bit scared to mess up. A neighbor called the other day asking if I wanted to go golfing. The timing was off, I had something else to do. But I was afraid if I said "no", the invitation might not come again. I know there are men's groups I could join, there are rotary clubs and church activities that are calling my name. The road to travel this **F** is uncharted territory, this place of fun and friends has been limited. Maybe I'll join the wrong groups or realize that I don't like golfing that much after all. Maybe I'll have nothing in common with the people in the men's club or at church. Maybe I'll find that I don't know how to give of myself emotionally or that I don't know how to accept a friendship.

But I can tell you this: My pad of paper is coming out. I will define the small steps I need to take to give it my all, to find the places where friendships live, and to find what brings me joy and comfort.

* * *

Perhaps you are surprised to learn that something as seemingly intuitive as having fun and having friends would be so difficult for some, like me. Maybe you know what is enjoyable but are still looking for the types of lasting and meaningful friendships. Or possibly, you've got this value perfectly balanced. While this chapter is literally about allowing fun and friendships to enter your life, it's also about the "beginner's mind" of approaching something new and scary...even late in life. There is always new work to do to try to balance the areas that you've devoted less energy. It's never too late to start, it's never too late to master something you've not yet accomplished.

Fun/Friends: *Use this section to understand the role of friends and fun in your life. Below are thought-starter questions. Answer these, or other questions that feel more relevant.*

Do you consider yourself someone who needs a lot of friends?

_____

_____

_____

_____

What traits do you value most in a friend? Do you feel you have these qualities?

_____

_____

_____

_____

What activities do you do with your friends that bring you the most joy?

_____

_____

_____

_____

If you could design the perfect day, what would it look like?

_____

_____
_____
_____

Why is fun important to you?

_____
_____
_____
_____

Chapter 12
THE SIXTH F

Looking back through these past fifty plus years, I ask myself what really has made my life work when it did and what were the common issues when the challenges overwhelmed me? What works for me, and what I've learned to come back to time and again are the **5 Fs** While they cannot all be equally important at all times, and perhaps they don't need to be, they all play a role in the fabric of my life.

FAMILY

FAITH

FORTUNE

FITNESS

FUN/FRIENDS

It wasn't until I reached the end of this book that I realized there is really a sixth **F**: Fulfillment. I have shared my story, not necessarily for you to simply read about my trials, but rather for you to gain strength and direction from my journey. Throughout this book, I have given testimony to the **5 Fs** and the importance they have played in my life. At the end of every section, I've intentionally asked questions so that you can define these values in your own way to begin the process of incorporating them into your life.

What I've learned most is that if I give either too much or too little attention to any of the **Fs**, my world tilts to a place of pain, or discomfort at the very least. Balanced, they bring me incredible fulfillment. Years ago, I learned that working too much did not allow for the other **Fs** in my life, so I needed to find a way to achieve the career success I wanted, but not lose sight of the other **Fs**. I learned that when I lean away from my Family, I feel lost, when I bend in towards my Faith, I find meaning, when I focus too much on my Fortune, I lose balance, when I ignore my

Fitness, I get sick, when I forget about Fun, my world is empty.

Being able to identify which **F** is out of alignment is critical; taking small steps to correct the direction is also essential. Four O'clock Fridays was the first step I took. I'm a long way from taking my last.

What I hope is that at the end of my life, when my family and friends do write that eulogy, the words I once hoped would comprise my homage will indeed be the truth of the way I lived my life and the way I impacted those who matter most.

Acknowledgments

During a speaking engagement at Auburn University, a student whose name I will never know approached me after the session. With emotion in his voice, he told me that he had heard me speak last time I was on campus, and that my words had had a significant impact on his life. As he walked away, it struck me that several other people had told me similar things. It was at that moment that I realized I wanted to write a book.

Months later, over a casual lunch, the book was born. My deepest gratitude goes out to Suzy Mayer who was able to take the words and stories of my life and translate them into the meaningful experiences and learnings of this book. The many iterations until it reached the exact state of representation taught each of us more than we ever expected.

I am beyond grateful to Kim Wayman whose impassioned dedication to brilliant editing for both content and grammar took the work to another level. Kim also designed the book cover, translating perfectly the essence of the themes into design.

A special thank you to Malcolm Bruni for reading with an open mind and offering insight, perspective and encouragement.

Thank you to my friend Doug Reader who was intuitive enough to understand what I needed at a time when I was hanging by a thread.

Thank you to Ray, Joan, and Jeff for leading by example and showing me complete family affection.

Thank you to my colleagues, my bosses, my teammates for pushing me when warranted, working with me in partnership when needed, and believing in me when justified. Each of you have made an impression on my character.

Lastly, and most importantly, thank you to my wife Jill and my boys who have given unconditional love, who have given greater meaning to my life and who have made me want to be a better man. I am proud of each of you; you mean everything to me.

119

Made in the USA
Columbia, SC
24 February 2020